CELEBRATING FATHERHOOD *with the* PROPHETS

CELEBRATING FATHERHOOD *with the* PROPHETS

COMPILED BY SHELLY LOCKE
ARTWORK BY ANNE MARIE OBORN

CFI · AN IMPRINT OF CEDAR FORT, INC. · SPRINGVILLE, UTAH

ISBN 13: 978-1-4621-2345-2

Published by CFI, an imprint of Cedar Fort, Inc.
2373 W. 700 S., Springville, UT 84663
Distributed by Cedar Fort, Inc., www.cedarfort.com

Library of Congress Control Number: 2019937874

Cover design by Shawnda T. Craig
Interior layout and design by Shawnda T. Craig

Edited by Nicole Terry and Kaitlin Barwick

Printed in Canada

10 9 8 7 6 5 4 3 2 1

Printed on acid-free paper

Dedicated to

my father; to my husband, Brian, the father of our children; and to the fathers of the prophets whose sterling example, strength of character, dedicated leadership, and righteous influence have been a source of inspiration for millions.

—Shelly

“The sacred title of

‘FATHER’

is shared with the Almighty.”

—President Ezra Taft Benson

Contents

"Words and language
are inadequate to express the
GRATITUDE
THAT I OWE TO GOD
for having given me
so honorable a parentage."

—Prophet Joseph Smith

“I LOVE MY FATHER

and his memory; and the memory of his noble deeds rests with ponderous weight upon my mind, and many of his **KIND AND PARENTAL WORDS** to me are written on the tablet of my heart."

—PROPHET JOSEPH SMITH

"I have remembered scenes
of my childhood.
**I HAVE THOUGHT
OF MY FATHER . . .**
He was of noble stature
and possessed a high, and holy,
and exalted, and virtuous mind."

—Prophet Joseph Smith

"IT IS FOR THE HUSBAND TO LEARN HOW

to gather around his family the comforts of life, how to control his passions and temper, and how to command the respect, not only of his family but of all his brethren, sisters and friends."

—Prophet Brigham Young

“The father should be

FULL OF KINDNESS,

and endeavor to

HAPPIFY AND CHEER

the mother, that her heart may
be comforted and her affections
unimpaired in her earthly protector,

THAT HER LOVE FOR GOD AND RIGHTEOUSNESS may vibrate throughout her whole being, that she may bear and bring forth offspring impressed and endowed with all the qualities necessary to a being designed to reign king of kings and lord of lords."

—PROPHET BRIGHAM YOUNG

"Let the husband and father learn to

BEND HIS WILL TO THE WILL OF HIS GOD,

and then instruct his [wife] and children in this lesson of self-government by his example as well as by precept, and his neighbor also, showing them how to be brave and steadfast. . . . Such a course as this will eventually subdue that unhallowed influence which works upon the human heart."

—Prophet Brigham Young

"If I . . . was the head of a family, I would want to **TEACH MY FAMILY RIGHT** and teach them the principles of virtue, holiness, purity, honor and integrity, that they might be worthy citizens, and that they might be able to stand before God, that when they and I get through this world, we might be worthy to meet the elect of God (those whom he has selected from the nations of the earth), and the Gods in the eternal world. Therefore, every morning, as head of my family, I should **DEDICATE MYSELF AND MY FAMILY TO GOD.**"

—Prophet John Taylor

"As man is an eternal being, and all his actions have a relevancy to eternity, it is necessary that he understand his position well, and thus

FULFIL THE MEASURE OF HIS CREATION:

for as he and his offspring are destined to live eternally, he is not only responsible for his own acts, but, in a great measure, for those of his children; in training their minds, regulating their morals, setting them a correct example,

AND TEACHING THEM CORRECT PRINCIPLES."

—Prophet John Taylor

"GOD IS OUR FATHER; WE ARE HIS CHILDREN.

He has brought us into his covenant and it is our privilege to go on from wisdom to wisdom, from intelligence to intelligence, from understanding of one principle to that of another, to go forward and progress in the development of truth until we can comprehend God, for we are his children; we are his sons and daughters; and he is our Father."

—PROPHET JOHN TAYLOR

"The man stands at the head of the family. He is the patriarch of his household. . . . There is no more beautiful sight on earth than to see a man stand at the head of his family and teach them righteous principles and give them good counsel.

These children honor their father, and they take **CONSOLATION AND JOY IN HAVING A FATHER WHO IS A RIGHTEOUS MAN."**

—Prophet Wilford Woodruff

"How important it is that we should

BE WISE FATHERS . . .

and that we should act wisely in instilling into their youthful minds all those principles that will lead them to that which is just, and to carry out in their lives the principles of righteousness and truth . . .

Any man's mind that is open and who looks forward to the work that lies before us, will

SEE AND FEEL

that the responsibility that rests upon him concerning his own family, and especially in the rearing up of his children,

IS VERY GREAT."

—Prophet Wilford Woodruff

"You go into a family where a man treats his wife and children kindly, and you will find that they will treat him in the same way. . . .

WE SHOULD BE KIND TO ONE ANOTHER,

do good to one another, and labor to promote the welfare, the interest and the happiness of each other, especially those of our own households."

—PROPHET WILFORD WOODRUFF

"It becomes the duties of fathers in Israel to wake up and become saviors of men, that they may walk before the Lord in that strength of faith, and that determined energy that will insure them the inspiration of the Almighty to **TEACH THE WORDS OF LIFE TO THEIR FAMILIES."**

—Prophet Lorenzo Snow

"It is the business of the father to be

QUALIFIED TO TEACH AND INSTRUCT HIS CHILDREN,

and to lay principles before them, so that by conforming to those instructions they can be the most happy that their natures are susceptible of in a state of childhood, while at the same time **THEY LEARN THE PRINCIPLES** upon which they can gain the most happiness and enjoyment in a state of manhood."

—Prophet Lorenzo Snow

"The men ought to be more fatherly at home, possessing finer feelings in reference to their wives and children, . . . more kindly and godlike. When I go into a family I do admire to see the head of that family administering to it as a man of God, kind and gentle, filled with the Holy Ghost and with the **WISDOM AND UNDERSTANDING OF HEAVEN.**"

—Prophet Lorenzo Snow

"WHAT THEN IS THE IDEAL HOME—MODEL HOME, such as it should be the ambition of the Latter-day Saints to build . . . ? It is one in which all worldly considerations are secondary. One in which the father is devoted to the family with which God has blessed him, counting them of first importance, and in which they in turn permit him to live in their hearts. One in which there is **CONFIDENCE, UNION, LOVE, SACRED DEVOTION BETWEEN FATHER AND MOTHER AND CHILDREN AND PARENTS."**

—Prophet Joseph F. Smith

“MAY THE FATHERS IN ISRAEL LIVE AS THEY SHOULD LIVE;

treat their wives as they should treat them; make their homes as comfortable as they possibly can; lighten the burden upon their companions as much as possible; set a proper example before their children;

teach them to meet with them in prayer,
morning and night, and whenever they sit down
to partake of food, to acknowledge
the mercy of God in giving them the food that
they eat and the raiment that they wear, and

ACKNOWLEDGE THE HAND OF GOD IN ALL THINGS."

—PROPHET JOSEPH F. SMITH

"There is no higher authority in matters relating to the family organization, and especially when that organization is presided over by one holding the higher Priesthood, than that of the father. The authority is time honored, and among the people of God in all dispensations it has been highly respected and often emphasized by the teachings of the prophets who were inspired of God. . . . **EVERY FATHER SHOULD RISE TO THE DIGNITY OF HIS HOLY OFFICE AS HEAD OF HIS FAMILY."**

—PROPHET JOSEPH F. SMITH

Preach My Gospel

"The best inheritance that you can leave to your sons and daughters is an **INVESTMENT IN THE KINGDOM OF GOD.**"

—Prophet Heber J. Grant

"I know nothing of course of the advice and counsel of a father because mine died when I was a baby, but I have learned of his reputation from others. People assure me that Jedediah M. Grant

WAS ONE OF THE NOBLEMEN OF THIS CHURCH. . . .

I am mentioning [this] in the hope that parents will realize that the example of integrity, of devotion, of loyalty to the Gospel, and the disposition not to find fault, but to labor diligently and unceasingly for the advancement of truth, is a

MARVELOUS HERITAGE TO LEAVE THEIR CHILDREN."

—Prophet Heber J. Grant

“EVERY FATHER WHO LOVES THE GOSPEL is ready and willing to go to the ends of the earth to preach it, and one of the greatest joys that any man can have is to be found in bringing souls to a knowledge of the truth. It ought to be a greater joy to us to train our children in the plan of salvation.”

—PROPHET HEBER J. GRANT

"I want to suggest to you . . . , there is no time that you can spend, no way in which you can utilize your time that will be of greater advantage than **TRAINING YOUR BOYS AND YOUR GIRLS TO BE WORTHY** of the blessings of our Heavenly Father."

—Prophet George Albert Smith

"I WONDER SOMETIMES IF AS FATHERS

we take pains to explain to our boys the seriousness of the obligation assumed when a boy becomes a deacon.

I wonder if when the boy is ordained
a deacon the father lets him feel that
he has something now that is

ETERNALLY IMPORTANT . . .

I had the matter so presented to
me and the importance of it,
that I felt it was a great honor."

—Prophet George Albert Smith

"Let us commit ourselves to the principle and the practice of gathering our families around us in our own homes. Let each one of us ask himself:

'HAVE I DONE MY DUTY IN MY HOME in reading and in teaching the gospel, as it has been revealed through the prophets of the Lord? Have I kept my children close to me and made home a pleasant place and a place of reverence, love, understanding, and devotion? . . .'

OUR CHILDREN ARE THE MOST PRECIOUS GIFT that our Father bestows upon us. If we can guide their feet in the pathway of salvation, there will be joy eternal for us and for them."

—PROPHET GEORGE ALBERT SMITH

"I ask tonight that every father in the Church see to it that in all sincerity he impress his children with the reality of the existence of God and with the reality that

GOD WILL GUIDE AND PROTECT HIS CHILDREN.

You carry that responsibility."

—PROPHET DAVID O. MCKAY

"No other success can compensate
for failure in the home.
The poorest shack in which
LOVE PREVAILS
over a united family
is of greater value to God

and future humanity than any other riches. In such a home **GOD CAN WORK MIRACLES** and will work miracles."

—PROPHET DAVID O. MCKAY

"If you would have
your child live a life
of virtue, of self-control,
of good report, then set him a

WORTHY EXAMPLE

in all these things."

—PROPHET DAVID O. MCKAY

"**FATHERS** can provide no greater leadership in the kingdom of God than to **LEAD THEIR FAMILIES** in holding family home evenings. When such experiences are a part of home life there builds up a unity and family respect which influence each person toward increased righteousness and happiness."

—Prophet Joseph Fielding Smith

"I hope that you are **TEACHING YOUR CHILDREN** in your homes **TO PRAY**. I hope that you are having family prayers, morning and evening, that your children are taught by example and by precept to observe the **COMMANDMENTS THAT ARE SO PRECIOUS** and so sacred and mean so much to our salvation in the kingdom of God."

—Prophet Joseph Fielding Smith

"We have been trying to impress
upon parents the need of
**PAYING MORE ATTENTION
TO THEIR CHILDREN,**
having a little more of the spirit
of the gospel in their homes,
a little more unity and a little more faith;
a little more responsibility
on the part of the fathers."

—PROPHET JOSEPH FIELDING SMITH

"Strengthen your family ties and
BE MINDFUL OF YOUR CHILDREN. . . .
Be sure that the home is made the strong place to which children can come for the anchor they need in this day of trouble and turmoil. Then love will abound and your joy will be increased."

—PROPHET HAROLD B. LEE

“The greatest work you brethren will ever do as fathers will be within the walls of your own home. . . .

DRAW YOUR CHILDREN AROUND ABOUT YOU.

TEACH THEM, GUIDE THEM AND GUARD THEM. There was never a time when we needed so much the strength and the solidarity of the home."

—PROPHET HAROLD B. LEE

"If a father's love for his sons is strong, and from their infancy he has taken them into his arms in loving embrace and let them feel the warmth of his affection for them, I believe that such comradeship will ripen with maturity and keep them near when a crisis in the boy's life requires the steadying hand of a

FATHER WHO UNDERSTANDS."

—PROPHET HAROLD B. LEE

"Constant training, constant vigilance, companionship, and being watchmen of our own children are necessary in order to keep our homes intact and to

BLESS OUR CHILDREN

in the Lord's own way."

—Prophet Spencer W. Kimball

"Certainly if fathers are to be respected, they must merit respect—if they are to be loved, they must be **CONSISTENT, LOVABLE, UNDERSTANDING, AND KIND . . .**

They must see themselves as
fortunate trustees of precious
spirit children whom
**GOD HAS
ENTRUSTED** for their care."

—Prophet Spencer W. Kimball

"Fathers and mothers, your foremost responsibility is your family. By working together you can have the kind of home the Lord expects you to have. **BY SHOWING LOVE AND CONSIDERATION** for one another and for your children, you can build a reservoir of spiritual strength that will never run dry."

—PROPHET SPENCER W. KIMBALL

“THE SACRED TITLE
OF ‘FATHER’
is shared with the Almighty. …
Our pattern or model for
fatherhood is our Heavenly Father.”

—PROPHET EZRA TAFT BENSON

"Fatherhood is not a matter of
station or wealth; it is a matter of
DESIRE, DILIGENCE, AND DETERMINATION
to see one's family exalted
in the celestial kingdom. . . .

God bless all the fathers in Israel to do well the work within the walls of our own homes. With the Lord's help

WE SHALL SUCCEED

in this, our most important responsibility."

—PROPHET EZRA TAFT BENSON

“FATHERHOOD IS LEADERSHIP,

the most important kind of leadership. It has always been so; it will always be so.”

—Prophet Ezra Taft Benson

"A righteous father **PROTECTS HIS CHILDREN** with his time and presence in their social, educational, and spiritual activities and responsibilities."

—PROPHET HOWARD W. HUNTER

"A man who holds the priesthood regards the family as ordained of God. Your leadership of the family is your most important and

SACRED RESPONSIBILITY.

THE FAMILY is the most important unit in time and in eternity and, as such, transcends every other interest in life."

—PROPHET HOWARD W. HUNTER

“Tender expressions of love and affection toward children are as much the responsibility of the father as the mother.

TELL YOUR CHILDREN YOU LOVE THEM.”

—Prophet Howard W. Hunter

"We speak with our earthly father.
He is our dear friend,
OUR PROTECTOR,
the one who usually supplies our
food and clothing and home."

—Prophet Gordon B. Hinckley

"I have chosen to speak
to the **FATHERS . . .**
In terms of your happiness,
in terms of the matters that
make you **PROUD** or sad,

nothing—I repeat, nothing—
will have so profound an
effect on you as the way
YOUR CHILDREN
turn out."

—Prophet Gordon B. Hinckley

“GOD BLESS YOU, DEAR FATHERS.

May He bless you with wisdom and judgment, with understanding, with self-discipline and self-control, with faith and kindness and love. And may He bless the sons and daughters who have come into your homes, that yours may be a fortifying, strengthening, guiding hand as they walk the treacherous path of life.”

—PROPHET GORDON B. HINCKLEY

"THE TRAINING OF OUR OWN FAMILIES requires our presence, our time, our best efforts. To be effective in our training, we must be stalwart in our examples to our family members and available for private time with each member, as well as time for counseling and guidance."

—PROPHET THOMAS S. MONSON

"If any parent needs added inspiration to commence his God-given teaching task, let him remember that the

MOST POWERFUL COMBINATION OF EMOTIONS

in the world is not called out by any grand cosmic event nor found in novels or history books—but merely by a parent gazing down upon a sleeping child.

That glorious biblical passage,

'CREATED IN THE IMAGE OF GOD,'

will acquire new and vibrant meaning as a parent repeats this experience. Home will become a haven called heaven, and loving parents will teach their children 'to pray, and to walk uprightly before the Lord' (D&C 68:28)."

—Prophet Thomas S. Monson

"Fathers, I would counsel you to demonstrate love and kindness to your wife.

BE PATIENT WITH YOUR CHILDREN.

Don't indulge them to excess, for they must learn to make their own way in the world. I would encourage you to be available to your children. I have heard it said that no man, as death approaches, has ever declared that he wished he had spent more time at the office."

—Prophet Thomas S. Monson

Artwork

by Anne Marie Oborn

References

Introductory quote by Ezra Taft Benson
Ezra Taft Benson, "Great Things Required of Their Fathers," *Ensign*, May 1981.

Joseph Smith

1. "Chapter 42: Family: The Sweetest Union for Time and for Eternity," *Teachings of Presidents of the Church: Joseph Smith* (2011), 485.
2. "Chapter 42: Family: The Sweetest Union for Time and for Eternity," 484.
3. "Chapter 42: Family: The Sweetest Union for Time and for Eternity," 483.

Brigham Young

1. *Discourses of Brigham Young*, sel. John A. Widtsoe (Salt Lake City, UT: Deseret Book, n.d.), 198.
2. *Discourses of Brigham Young*, 198–99.
3. *Discourses of Brigham Young*, 198.

John Taylor

1. "Chapter 21: Strengthening Families," *Teachings of Presidents of the Church: John Taylor* (2011), 195–96.
2. "Chapter 21: Strengthening Families," 195.
3. Emerson Roy West, *Latter-day Prophets: Their Lives, Teachings, and Testimonies and Profiles of Their Wives* (American Fork, UT: Covenant Communications, 1999), 45.

Wilford Woodruff

1. "Chapter 16: Marriage and Parenthood: Preparing Our Families for Eternal Life," *Teachings of Presidents of the Church: Wilford Woodruff* (2011), 168–69.
2. "Chapter 16: Marriage and Parenthood: Preparing Our Families for Eternal Life," 167–68.
3. "Chapter 16: Marriage and Parenthood: Preparing Our Families for Eternal Life," 168.

Lorenzo Snow

1. C. J. Williams, ed., *Teachings of Lorenzo Snow* (Salt Lake City, UT: Bookcraft, 1996), 135.
2. C. J. Williams, 134.
3. C. J. Williams, 135.

Joseph F. Smith

1. "Chapter 20: The Eternal Union of Husband and Wife," *Teachings of Presidents of the Church: Joseph F. Smith* (2011), 180.
2. "Chapter 43: Fathers in the Home," *Teachings of Presidents of the Church: Joseph F. Smith* (2011), 385.
3. "Chapter 43: Fathers in the Home," 383.

Heber J. Grant

1. *Teachings of the Presidents of the Church: Heber J. Grant* (2011), 204.
2. "Chapter 22: Teaching Children in the Nurture and Admonition of the Gospel," *Teachings of Presidents of the Church: Heber J. Grant* (2011), 206–7.
3. "Chapter 22: Teaching Children in the Nurture and Admonition of the Gospel," 202.

George Albert Smith

1. "Chapter 22: Bringing Up Children in Light and Truth," *Teachings of Presidents of the Church: George Albert Smith* (2011), 238.
2. "Chapter 5: The Holy Priesthood—for the Blessing of God's Children," *Teachings of Presidents of the Church: George Albert Smith* (2011), 45.
3. "Chapter 22: Bringing Up Children in Light and Truth," 241.

David O. McKay

1. *Gospel Ideals: Selections from the Discourses of David O. McKay* (Salt Lake City: Improvement Era Publication, 1953), 483.
2. In Conference Report, April 1964, 5.
3. In Conference Report, April 1955, 27.

Joseph Fielding Smith

1. "Chapter 16: Bringing Up Children in Light and Truth," *Teachings of Presidents of the Church: Joseph Fielding Smith* (2011), 211.
2. "Chapter 16: Bringing Up Children in Light and Truth," 210.
3. "Chapter 4: Strengthening and Preserving the Family," *Teachings of Presidents of the Church: Joseph Fielding Smith* (2011), 80.

Harold B. Lee

1. "Chapter 14: Love at Home," *Teachings of Presidents of the Church: Harold B. Lee* (2011), 131.
2. In Conference Report, April 1973, 130.
3. "Chapter 14: Love at Home," 134.

Spencer W. Kimball

1. "Chapter 19: Strengthening Our Families," *Teachings of Presidents of the Church: Spencer W. Kimball* (2011), 206.
2. *The Teachings of Spencer W. Kimball* (Salt Lake City, UT: Bookcraft, 1982).
3. Spencer W. Kimball, "The Example of Abraham," *Ensign*, June 1975, 3.

Ezra Taft Benson

1. *The Teachings of Ezra Taft Benson* (Salt Lake City, UT: Bookcraft, 1988), 503.
2. "Great Things Required of Their Fathers," *Ensign*, May 1981.
3. "Chapter 15: The Sacred Callings of Fathers and Mothers," *Teachings of Presidents of the Church: Ezra Taft Benson* (2011), 194.

Howard W. Hunter

1. "Being a Righteous Husband and Father," *Ensign*, Nov. 1994.
2. "Being a Righteous Husband and Father."
3. "Being a Righteous Husband and Father."

Gordon B. Hinckley

1. "You Are a Child of God," *Ensign*, May 2003.
2. "'Great Shall Be the Peace of Thy Children,'" *Ensign*, Nov. 2000.
3. "'Great Shall Be the Peace of Thy Children.'"

Thomas S. Monson

1. "Heavenly Homes, Forever Families," *Ensign*, June 2006, 99–100.
2. "Only a Teacher," *Ensign*, Jan. 1990.
3. "Constant Truths for Changing Times," *Ensign*, May 2005, 20.

About Anne Marie

ANNE MARIE OBORN

A painting may evoke joy, unveil truth, or enliven the soul. Color harmony and quality of light are characteristic of Anne Marie's sensitive portraits, sunlit florals, and bravura landscapes. She has received numerous awards, including the *Permalba Paint Award* granted through the *Oil Painters of America National Show*, of which she is a signature member.

Anne Marie's husband, Garth, is also a recognized artist. They have four children and reside in Bountiful, Utah. Anne Marie's work may also be purchased at the *Southam Gallery* in Salt Lake City, Utah. You can find out more about Anne Marie and her artwork online at www.anneoborn.com.

About Shelly

SHELLY LOCKE is an international advocate for motherhood. For over a decade, her advocacy has taken her by invitation to many nations of the world, speaking to policymakers, leaders and mothers alike regarding the vital contribution mothers make to their countries.

Shelly served as the Utah Young Mother of the Year as well as representing Utah at the White House. Her educational background is founded in social work and early childhood development with a specialty in mother-child attachment. Shelly is passionate about the well-being of mothers and the children they love.